Stumble Into a Lighted Room

poems by

Bill Buege

Dan,

Many thanks,

Bill Buege

Stumble Into a Lighted Room

Published by Burlesque Press
www.burlesquepressllc.com

ISBN: 978-0-9964850-5-0

Book design by Daniel Wallace

to Mary Anne

Grateful acknowledgment is made to the editors and publishers of the following magazines and journals in which the indicated poems first appeared:

Callaloo, "Unafraid" (former title: "Michael")
First Things, "Change"
Gambling the Aisle, "Arrested," "School"
Garbanzo, "6 Stages of Old Age"
Liquid Squid, "The Normal Curve"
Meat for Tea: The Valley Review, "Hatred"
Plainsong, "Nebraska Woman"
Riprap, "Fixed on Zombies"
River Styx, "She Swept the Abattoir" (former title: "Mom")
Sou'wester, "Sun City"
The Sow's Ear, "Ribbon" (former title: "Ursula")
Step Away, "Life in a Seashell"

The following poems appeared in the privately published *Imitations*: "Divorce," "The Man Mouth," "A Simple Man."

Darrell Seibel provided the historical documents that are the basis for the Kansas section of poems.

Dr. Ed and Marie Schroeder helped me with the German in "Guten Morgen" but are not responsible for any errors in the poem.

Table of Contents

Part One:

Kansas

Air sweet with grass

So you got here because your parents did,
and they because of theirs,
and now you watch the sky turn pale around the edge
and black above before the stars come out,
and hear the grass and feel the evening breeze soft on your face.
All that and more because your great great grandad stopped,
decided he had seen enough, that this was beautiful enough
for him and his, which means, for you,
far from everything, from edges, ends, from oceans,
mountains, cities full of humans' words and jealousy.
You're free to watch the ants traipse back and forth,
to think about the flowering grass, to dream yourself
an older you with little girls who run about the yard,
skip rope, and call out, "Mama, quick, come see the bug."

The sun just up

She came west to Fort Hays,
became a captain's maid,
spilled on herself
a pot of boiling water,
died at nineteen.
One second a young maid,
then madness, death.
Between, boiling water
spilling from a pot.
The Fort Hays record shows
many died of fever,
syphilis, accident.
Death proves the best hope
the not-famous have
for a place in history.

George Armstrong Custer deserts his command

The tall grass knelt to me, whispered a hymn
too soft to recognize. The night wind played
the cottonwoods, a million tiny chimes.
I heard one word, your name, Elizabeth,
while all across the river slept in night.
Then north I saw you riding on the sky,
alabaster white beneath the midnight moon
We raced together, silent, for some hours.
You turned to me, a teardrop on your cheek,
sighed, sad as a mother of ten dead sons,
whistled Garry Owen as if a hundred Sioux
surrounded us and we were bound for death.
Then off you flew across the setting moon
and east into the predawn sky, followed
by your cry, "Aiee. Come with me, dear man.
Forever." To simple river song I rode.
I do not honor life or uniform
one half as much as I love you, Elizabeth.

Nice people

I lost words first,
last the pictures in my head.
Not much left inside
eat, sleep, vomit, hide
until the lady
thirty miles west
gets cooked on her hearth,
when words creep back
and fearsome images
pierced, quartered,
bludgeoned, flayed,
blinded, skinned,
eviscerated.

It is so beautiful

The wind rose, the clouds flew.
It froze, then snowed all night,
all day, into the second night.
Come dawn, snow lay three quarters
up my window panes,
the sky empty of everything but sky,
the temperature so low I felt I lived
inside a crystal bell
where any movement,
a wisp of wind across a stem of grass,
would deafen me.
Later, I heard the river ice a half mile away.
Later, a deer foraging.
I went outside. My snow shoes fired
ten gauge shotgun shells.
The second empty night the horse froze
where he stood soundlessly, while ten
million stars lit his final hours.
I woke the second morning,
walked toward the river.
Halfway, I crossed the footpaths of
a dozen men and horses passing south.

The grass blue and wet

White folk hung them in a gully,
three black bluecoats
who shot the wrong man
in a Hays saloon.
Rope snapped three necks.
We do not know
the vigilantes' children never knew.
Next generation killed
enough to end a war.
Drought returned to Kansas.
The past is easy pickings
choose the words, photographs, songs,
while minute by minute hours disappear.
Wet of dew, incontinence, blood.
Blue of blue-black Africans,
sky, soldiers' clothes, veins
that break in rope-stretched necks.

The air so fresh it's like we're new born

Unless we aren't in now,
some now occurred in
some time then, some when
when humans were not yet,
nor animals, nor birds,
when all was only full fresh air,
and full fresh earth, wind,
ancient sun and frozen moon, rain,
when no lines marked
a map to represent
a piece of land,
no one named a river,
defined a plat.
All lay innocent
of human mind,
In that fourth creation day
half a billion years ago
god dozed, and dazzled
by a dream, conceived a you.

The soldiers' women ... wander the Great American Desert

You understand how close we are to nothingness:
how brave the props in lush abundance,
manmade things and dreams of things,
piles of thoughts, recombinant words,
painted canvases, metal copies of ourselves,
billions rolls of exposed celluloid,
forks and pots, bowls and souvenirs
of Yellowstone, junkyards rich in carcasses.
How marvelous the set that changes by itself,
mountains risen from the sea to wear away
to hills, torrential rivers eating at their beds,
winds that shape, reshape the center of a continent.
Endless this play. A few lines, some fun,
a child, the ax, our exit back into the audience.
How dark the theatre, the spectators,
the empty seats we take among the staring shades.

Do you suppose they make sense of the endless highway?

I watch the earth move through
the houses of the zodiak,
the moon turn full, then die,
the poles turn to and from the sun.

House shadows pull into themselves,
fat men sucking in their bellies,
let go, until they blend with night
and disappear.

The moon draws up the oceans,
lets them return,
while wind shapes waves,
men stand, then sit, then sleep.

Rhythms are the breath of earth.
All things expand and shrink,
turn in harmony,
replenishing their energy

save human minds
that take apart the watch God made
and pile up the parts,
in love with parts and speed.

Part Two:

The Man in Red Flannel Union Suit

She swept the abattoir at night

My mom came home smelling
like blood sausage, ripe hamburger,
sheep brains, woke us, showered,

walked out in her bra and panties, wet hair
in a red bandana. She fried us eggs
in butter, made us toast, fixed our lunch

before she went to bed. I hear her,
see her wet back and cotton underwear.
Whenever I smell blood, I think sex.

Fixed on Zombies

Immortality attracts us all.
The schoolboy thinks: If I knew I lived forever,
I would refuse to fold my hands in church.
I'd say mean things about our priest,

crawl from my grave, stuff my face with Skittles,
and head down to our skateboard park.

His father thinks: If I were a zombie,
I would suck my neighbor's blood instead of watching
football on TV.

His mother thinks: I'd frighten little kids,
watch my girlfriends rise from graves
refreshed by night, the moon, the time of year,
frost on their hair.
I'd greet them with a zombie kiss,
and off we'd go.

The timid poet thinks: If I came from the underworld,
I'd lick my scars,
hobble to the toughest neighborhood in town,
kill everyone,
and hunt for virgins in their bedroom.

The zombie thinks: If I were human,
I'd be a gentle man.
I would treat my wife and children with respect,
would never speak an angry word to anyone.

Poetaster

I count the maze of possibilities
Beneath the jeans, shirts, blouses, T's
Who came to hear me read my art.

Afterward, we blur into pure, unholy
Fucking. My readings and the sex
Form one sweet motion. That's how

I get through nights when two or three
Sit in the audience, and I must act as if
I mattered and they were more than lonely

Humans who have stumbled on a lighted room.
What good am I? Three times divorced,
Adulterer by trade, pretender at real verse.

But I have found my place, my comedy,
And I will act it out.

Green Frog

I caught a green frog in the wet grass down by our lake.
It was a lively fellow, but I leapt on it, cupped it in my hands,
felt it squirm, felt it's cool skin alive against my palms.

I carried it to our kitchen, put it in a jelly jar while I
filled a giant kettle with cold water, put the kettle on our stove,
turned on the gas, got out the frog, and dumped him in.

Dad had told me, "You drop a frog in boiling water, it'll jump out.
Put it in cold water, then, gradually, heat it to boiling, he'll
forget to jump, and you'll have a cooked frog." I had to try.

My green frog swam around awhile, seemed at home. The water
in my pot was getting hot. I watched the frog slow down, pull
out a tiny bar of soap from somewhere by his back legs, turn on his
back,

and wash himself. "What!? He's making fun of me." I turned the gas
to high. I'd make that joker boil. He started to turn red, then,
in a strange little voice, said, "Come on in. The water's fine."

I thought, why not, took off my clothes, climbed up on the stove,
jumped in, and screamed.

The Normal Curve

Your tongue felt smooth as Dairy Queen that day.
I did not know that feelings danced or sang
until we came
as one long flame or breath. Or sin. What wrong,

what sin did we commit?
Relieved, we dressed, went back
into our sixth grade class, where everyone
except our teacher knew.

While others played 'I dare,'
we walked outside, into the trees, made love,
at least a sort of love, a kindness, air.

School

We sat in rows and learned
to think in rows and walked
in rows, described our world as rows
of good and evil men. We worked in rows
of cubicles. Who knows

what we'd be now if we
had told the officers
we would not charge the enemy
in rows. Of course,

we died in rows, and lie
in rows of careful graves.

The Man in Red Flannel Union Suit

Down the street in Boulder, Colorado, walks,
not Santa, but some crazy guy whose life has slipped
away since Viet Nam and all the stimulants involved
in the Great 60s when he was a young man about to head
for college, parties so lascivious he'd have a hard-on
walking to his Monday morning remedial writing class,

but that ain't how it went for him, who got a low draft number,
fitness training, free trip overseas, a rifle, new friends,
new food, new girls to screw, rambles in the gorgeous jungle,
wild animals, drugs, freedom to murder anyone suspected
of a variant creed, survival, and home to a vanilla life.

Somehow between then and now time passed in a parade
of beef-fattened veterans and girls on floats, American flags,
to hell with work, it was all shit anyway. On his way to now
he found his flannel underwear, thinks he looks like a flayed
VC in it, likes the idea, tells himself stories about a sharpened
bowie knife, ears strung on a necklace, a black night of hand

grenades rolled over corpse piles, and luck, all it took
was luck. He's content to have his cardboard box, food
enough to keep alive, winter shelter. He talks loudly
as he walks downtown. The man's become a character
in a college community. Students share their snacks with him.

Hatred

Paralyzed, I'm forced to watch you piss my face,
you who once said I lay beneath your heart.
Perhaps, you think I am so worthless I do not

deserve the appellation *enemy*, must take your
urine as if I were a garage wall. In fact, my nose
and palate remain refined. I note the piss you splash

into my mouth predicts your life and death better
than a mage's dream. At your urine's edge I scent
the bitterness of bad Pinot, the garlic of cheap

Subway bread. Deeper, I taste serious disease.
Your liver no longer survives to cleanse your blood.
Your piss bouquet reveals a cancer. Prostate?

Perhaps. Or is it in your testicles? Hmm. I savor
the thick angina that adds its heady overtones. I may
be a weed to you, but soon you will lie under me.

Wittol

My mistress shares her gifts with many men
and women, too, she tells me, surprising me,
until she lets me watch. I stare and learn
how delicate men are, how easily
they lose their focus, die. The women are
more taken by the act, as if the coupling
not the end were all. They want much more,
are more at ease with flesh, more patient making
love in all love's ways. One man loved well.
I watched my mistress' eyes turn soft, unfocus
as he entered her. I watched her lips fill
full with blood and heard her moan and curse.
I learned what bumblers untrained lovers are.

Divorce

We sat together an autumn day
at a corner table in the Stag and Bear
and stared at our food that was lying there
among unspoken words. You were gray

with pain and our lies as we came to the end
but held to yourself, refused to say
what I wanted said. I watched you play
with your fork and your spoon and tend

to the lavender flowers and push at your food.
Wife, you had nothing to say, but I did.
I said it was time to divorce and hid
my thoughts about what was good

for me. You agreed, and we walked to our cars,
past the stag and the bear that time could not touch,
home to three little girls, and a dog, and such
legal affairs as were ours.

Fifty-Three Green Mercury

Night means sleep to me now I've grown old.
She's far away, a grandmother. We're homely
as two Holstein cows. My memory
confuses her with autumn's rusted gold,
something bold from Sappho's poetry,
a dried carnation in a diary.

Change

It had been her kitchen twenty years.
She put the ginger in the cupboard,
turned out the light, opened the back door.
The shattered globe of an old moon had spiked itself
along the blossoms on their dogwood tree.
He said it was over; therefore, it was over.
All solemn-eyed, naive, she drank him in,
his anger, standing there, hands on his hips,
watched him, practiced, redescribe their lives.
How well he's managing the separation.
It wasn't working. It couldn't. He couldn't.
Anymore.
They had lived together too long.
They were growing old together.
She sat on the stoop,
watched their cat sweep up and over the back fence
and the nickel-plated moon slip off their tree.
It was cooler, close to midnight.

The Pastor's Daughter

He can preach what he does not believe.
Years on years he calls his congregation to attend,

confesses vague sins, stokes their guilt with promises
of divine retribution. The child grows long limbed,
beautiful. He can no more keep his hands off her

than he can fail to wipe his shitty ass. His wife knows
that she should know more than she does, but dares

not ask. Pastor retires to a quiet life. His wife stays
with him, as does his daughter, who has reached
her middle age. A skinny woman, never married,

she keeps to herself, survives on drugs and hate,
does not know herself or what she should believe.
Each of us has one body, one mind, one life, one death.

The Meaning of Life

1. Words mean. Lives don't.

2. I wasted years reading the classics.
Now, I enjoy football on TV.

3. Congratulations, winner. You've just won.
You did it. Won.

4. Consider the lilies. They don't
do anything, but they have a caretaker.

5. Failure belongs to the game. You must fail
unless you refuse to play.

6. She had eleven pups. One died.
She grieved for it but still had ten.

7. I help the poor. And help myself.
Consequences? I live better.

8. Doctor gave himself to doctoring.
Preacher preached until he died.

9. You know, you write a poem
you really like, but no one takes it.

10. Some few succeed. What in hell
does that mean? Go away.

Last to Leave

Night is about to fade into dawn.
Elm tree leaves reflect a patient moon.
Soon the corner deli wakes.

  But not yet.
You are the last to leave,
   stand at their door.

She loved you back in college
   but she married him.

They stand beside each other, gently push you out
   with "Take care. We had a good time, too."

   You step onto their stoop.
   They close their door.

Their brownstone. Their gate. Their elm.

Part Three:

The Meadow

The Meadow

He carried her out to
the meadow, put her down,
and left. First, silence, then the buzz
of life, the morning sun,

the key that set the day
at ease. She smelled the song
of clover, heard the purple in
the cone flowers, felt the wings

of butterflies beat down
the air. A rabbit stared
at her, a mousing black snake paused,
and then, hunted by. No word

but grace, no thought but sky.
She did not mind Lord Sun,
sat motionless as billowed clouds
or larks. On the ground

the shade built walls for her,
an insubstantial home.
She did not wander in her mind
or think when he would come.

Life in a seashell

The trees on my street have been blooming for a week.
Down from my living room windows, the flower clouds grow.
Soon it will snow on our sidewalks and shoppers,
cabs and business men in expensive suits. Petals will drift
into grocery bags and bakery bags, onto warm loaves of Jewish rye,
cold chickens, palpable, heavy, wet in white butcher paper,
Greek olives in plastic containers and tins of English tea.
They will touch the back of the petty thief as he is pushed into the police

car.

Ribbon

Spring:
Praise god for pigs
that rut, snuffle, grunt,
that gallop out the front door
around and through the back,
that bury my spring violets in mud,
revert my court to swamp.
Spitted, their gristle snaps,
their fat spurts flamelets
out my chimney, distills,
lures the human swine into my sty
to drink my beer, eat, belch,
stink worse than a farting sow.
But short of pigs I'd starve.
Who'd visit Pigs on Spit
withouten pigs?

Summer:
Summer cooks my piggies
quicker than I'd choose.
But Pigs on Spit spurts on,
our chimney blacked with pig,
hot pig afloat the burning street.
In walks Jack. "Jack," I says,
"the regular?" "Yah," says he.
I slice a knuckle thick with crackling,
pour his beer, befoam my arm,
serve him up. He eats, says,

"Yer pig special sweet today.
You store her in the sun?"
He jokes, I'd guess,
considering his sense of fun,
but for movement of the bowel
ain't nothing like ripe pig.

Autumn:
This time of year I take account.
In all my while I've served
a mighty herd of swine, poured
troughs of beer down sour gullets,
burnt cords on cords of wood,
watched the ash rise.
How many hamhock hands have grabbed my bubs?
Four generations crawled
between my legs. As one they grunt
I'm ugly, hog fat, sin herself,
explode, pant, can't get enough of me,
make themselves swine for a slice of me.

Winter:
I got a new neighbor, a pie maker.
She makes her pies from anything,
meat, berries, roots, nuts. What's more, she buys
my fat, sometimes a roast hind quarter.
I tried her pie, bought some for Pigs on Spit,
decided to exchange roast pig for pie,
sat with her late last night, warm, by the spit,
watched snowflakes cake the window sill.

We hugged and said good night. She tells me what
a handsome one was I. I say, "Likewise."
She asks if I'd made love with women.
"No," I stammered. "Would you consider it?"
Clumsy as a child bride, I stumbled
up my stair with her. And she undressed me,
let me undress her. We kissed. Today,
the men look at me strange as if they know.
Or it may be the ribbon in my hair.

Those Damn Robins

Another winter, another batch of them.
They won't go south, think it will be warm

forever. They are so wrong. They flit
from yard to yard, grab bugs. Just wait.

One night it will freeze. They'll fluff
themselves in spruce trees, stay warm enough.

The clouds will clear, the brass hammer moon
hang still, sky fill with diamond nails, and down

will drop the gauge. Ground will harden,
air turn liquid. A few will hop out, gluttons

for pain, hungry, stupid. A few will
die. Most will huddle. Then comes the squall,

black sky, yards full of snow. One day I looked
into a January blizzard. A choke

cherry tree filled with robins reaching for frozen
cherries. Robins fell like ripe fruit, a dozen

wasted as rotting apples late in fall—
emblem of ignorance, evil, or nothing at all.

Gentle Heart

She watches from her room,
alone, content with dust mote
drift through cones of sun, plume

of lavender, silk coat
of Bach, English Breakfast tea.
Perhaps she'll dress her cat,

draw the orchard's breath. She
wraps herself in apple bloom
and pollinating bees.

Tricked by an early snow

I did not hear the snow.
I did not see the wind,
but when, at dawn, I looked outside,
I knew what I would find:

a white mound, once the barn,
an isolated tree,
and bluebirds scattered by the fence
like corpses in a war.

The birds lay fluffed with down,
protected from the storm.
Their uniforms of orange and blue
were lovely in the snow.

I bent to pick one up,
now frozen to the ground,
but light as air it pulled away,
a bluebell, on the wind.

Nebraska Woman

The ladder broke. She fell and broke her leg.
Two jagged ends of bone cut through her skin.
She lay alone, her cries for help unheard.
She had been painting in her second house,
redecorating for her renters. The living room
was dingy, needed work. And she knew how
to work. Always had. For years and years.
Was wealthy in her seventies. Peace and work,
what she needed now that she was old
and tough as a range chicken. She dragged herself
out the door and down the street. They found
her on the corner, bone splinters sticking from
her leg. Doctors bolted the bone to rods.
She learned to walk again, will let you feel
the nuts and screws, hard beneath her skin.

May Color Fishing

Day's catch: red-tailed hawk plume,
orange poppies, pumpkin day lilies,
last branch of redbud bloom,

two Monarch butterflies,
three purple irises, robin's
blue eggshell, turquoise skies,

teal thunder clouds (storm skin),
dust, butterscotch birch bark, dusk-loom
threaded fuchsia, cumin.

Two Ducklings at Rest on a Loon

And the fox crept down to the water.
The water crept out to the shore,
returned indifferent to what it heard:

heartbeat, electric-wave flow
through a sly brain, white teeth gnash
in a red-tongued, hungry mouth. Willows

cupped their ears at the water's edge,
listened for the plash of loon feet, haunt
of loon cry signaling a dying day.

And fox crept closer, sniffed the surface
of the lake, placed a fox foot
on the shore, waited. Ducklings,

your mama's corpse rests in the reeds.
Your father's flown south, left you
on the northern lake where you

were born and where your siblings,
little paddlers, were swallowed
by the pike that troll the coves.

Soon your lady loon must dive
for her late dinner. Listen to her cry
and to the water as it laps the shore.

You may hear the willows bend
to the midnight moon and the breathing
of the fox who waits for you.

Good Morning

A beautiful day, *ja*, Greta, *liebe Frau*.
The lindens on the boulevard reflect the dawn.
How sweet and blue the sky.

And you've set my perfect morning table:
Blutwurst, hard rolls, *Butterkäse*, a bowl
of *Spreewald Gurken*, black, black *Kaffee*.
Perhaps a drop of *Schnaps*.

You, dear one, fill my heart *mit Freude*.
Your beauty shines above Brunhild's.

This morning we shall stroll *Unter den Linden*,
proud Berliners, pushing baby Günther's *Kinderwagen*.

I have a secret I must share with you alone.
This is a very special day.
Come to your *Schatzi*. I will whisper it to you.

Our joy shall now be full.
Last night *der Führer* approved our plan.
Today we begin to exterminate the Jews.

Demon Mouse

Beside the trap,
its head chopped off.

A little blood and body fluid
glue it to the floor.

One year twelve mice lined up
at my traps. (This approaches

comedy.) Each was smaller
than the one before. Suicides?

Finally, I killed a baby,
cut in two by my trap wire.

We dream our demon mouse.

When I Have Died,

am turned to ashes in the undertaker's fire,
bottled in a decorated urn, handed to my
daughter's family; when they drive me

back to Omaha, and, after school is out,
to Ely, Minnesota, and the Blue Heron,
I will be home. At dawn they'll paddle

onto the lake. The water will reflect
the sky. The rice grass will pulse against
the dock. In the cove a blue heron

will wake, lift its head, watchful, still.
My daughter Meg will free me from my urn.
I'll make a pool of ashes on the water

while the sun stares, a silent loon floats by.
Perhaps, my kin will sing a song for me
as they watch me drift apart. Distracted

by their drive home and what they have
to do--their overgrown lawn, a garden
that needs tending, summer sports for Otto--

--they will leave me on the lake, alone,
to sink to the sand. Summer, fall
will pass. The lake will freeze. Wolves

will howl. Blue jays will scold. Mink
and chipmunks will settle in their dens.
Snowmobilers will drink by birch fires.

Arrested

At first I missed him there,
saw only browns and blacks.
I'd crossed their yard and back

without a thought that I
was trespassing, but, then,
I lived inside my head, had missed
the war. I had not seen

the children dressed like tramps
or heard the protest songs.
I did not note the Malcom X
in school yard blacks and browns.

The climb outside our town
is steep, the years fly by,
and I've become the favorite joke
folk tell when they're away.

Sun City

They carry their lives in worn golf bags
out their step-less houses to the golf course
from cool dawn to the hot months and the mountains.
Early morning, when dew tarnishes the grass,
wound-up baby quail run in lines through orange,
lemon, and grapefruit trees. Rabbits nibble
the small weeds along window sills. All day,
wrens pester the olive, and toward evening
the sky stacks with exercising birds
and bird calls. The only other sound,
from far away, clear, the ambulance siren.

Then one night police cordon off
a condominium on a golf course.
For a few black hours a photographer,
irritated at the double suicide,
catches in the flash of Cadillac headlamps.
Night comes so fast on the desert, which is why
at sunset the old people stay in,
prefer their fantasy of paradise
to the Eden they bought. But blue
cool evenings birds sing and call
and fly three hundred feet into the striated sky.

Part Four:

Today Is His Death Day

Cocaine Is Just a Word

for me. For you, dear child, it's life.
I do not know what happened

to our family. I do not know. What
happened? Cocaine, it's just a word

for me. For you, dear child, cocaine
became a way out of a tasteless place.

We could not find a way. Concrete
abutments held us on the way we rode.

That way was wrong for you. For me
it was a way. And I was young. You

were not born. I knew no way fit
what I wished to be. I knew you

before you left your mom. You knew
a better way before I left your mom.

Your way played dreams across
an empty sky. Such ways hold dandelion

seeds, cartwheels, the sweet breath
of a dress and patent leather shoes.

For me, dear child, cocaine is just a word.
For you, it tracks a trail back home.

(The emptiness of death)

The emptiness of death,
an afterthought. The road
there, pot-hole filled and curved,
ends sudden as it should.

Her bedding smells of her.
Her table holds her comb.
The sun shines through the window shades
and wakes her drowsing room,

but absence starts no birds,
means nothing to the day.
She left, a dandelion seed
blown silently away.

A Simple Man

A simple man, somewhat failed, somewhat old,
I find myself beside an empty hearth
and lose myself before no fire, no smoke,
no sparks that rise into our icy sky.
My cat curls by my head, unsheaths her claws
and growls, dreams of the mouse she will not catch,
decapitate, the bones she will not crush.
We are content with history and sleep:
one cat, one man, who dreams the milk blue sea,
the sun, islands of possibility.

You've read about the single-minded Jews
who wandered forty years outside the land
their god had promised them, and of the man
who sailed for home and would not be deterred
by goddesses or natural force. Nonsense.
No human lives one predetermined arc,
no group of men control the firmament.
We live as best we can through randomness,
alone. One day rhinoceroses run
down Main. One day men turn to swine. One day
one's wife decides he's not enough,
or someone finds one's darling worth the risk.
And everything is changed, and everyone.

Given drift, uncertainty, even in
the most familiar straits, I would not roam
to roam, rush forth merely to rush forth.

We have our cunning, fortune, home. That's all.
And I am home, though home is cold and still.

If I had men to follow me, I would
say, "No. Too much time's past. It is too late.
Stay home beside your cat. Enjoy your wife,
grandchildren, life, what life remains your hearth."
We were young. I doubt it pays to think on that
or on young women, passion. There's great gain.
They have no hold when sexual drives have waned.
They're like the snow that blows from icy streets.
To see a beautiful young woman, know
I cannot have her, ever, sets me free.
I have no need to join the pack of dogs
who circle round her heat, no need to try—
no need at all but sleep, a place to take
a good shit once a day, a chair, a cat.
I wonder why I bother with this pen,
these random lines composed in utter calm,
emotionless as chimes that mark the day,
dangerous as sleeping cats to mice,
memorable as failed men in empty rooms.

No Echoing Green

We wake and arise,
unaware of the skies
or the nurses who ring,
announce it is spring.
Old John thinks it's June
and he's going home soon.
We gather around
and wait for the sound
of our breakfast. This scene
is no echoing green.

Sweet Ann has no hair.
Bent Jim needs more care.
Poor Bob, once an oak,
sits and gobbles at folk.
Dear Emma will play
at whatever you say.
Her life, all her joys
are in flirting with boys,
old men who have seen
her undress on our green.

And I have grown weary
of laughing and merry
unknowns who descend
on my imminent end.
They tell me of mothers
and sisters and brothers,

upset my sweet nest.
Thank God, soon I'll rest
where I cannot be seen,
deep under the green.

Six Stages of Old Age

You've aged, become less flexible, grown softer.
Your day depends from what you meant to do.
Forget your pride. Old age begins with laughter.

You coaxed your wife to bed and tried to mount her,
lost your balance, grip, erection, knew
you'd aged, become less flexible, grown softer.

You thought you farted, did a good bit more,
squeezed your cheeks, and ran. It's easy to
forget your pride. Old age should fill with laughter.

One day your brand new dentures disappear.
No, they're in your mouth. Oh, shit, it's true,
you've aged, become forgetful, slower, softer,

but don't believe what's happening or care.
You're vanishing. No one remembers you
lived proud and strong. Old age should end in laughter.

You've chicken legs, a wattle like a rooster,
a pigeon's gait, a turkey brain. You coo
or gobble when you talk. You've aged, grown softer,
forgotten your first name, your pride, your laughter.

Unafraid

Spring:
I am told I am
a month from spring
but only a month
and that at noon
sun warms the south cathedral wall.
My room is cold,
though light seeps
through its high windows,
and it is my room,
my bed, my
doctor, who finds his way
into my street,
and my month until spring.

Summer:
He: You will not see another summer.
This thing in you grows toward your heart.
I: Summer filled my heart when I was young
and had two lovely boys, a gentle wife.
They predecease me. What matter days?
He: Soon you must have
your foretaste of hell.

Autumn:
My soul slips from me
these cool fall days
as I lie awake and dream.

I am of two realities,
a bed surrounded by a room,
a time somewhere when I
walk with my family,
fret what will become of us.
I wake again from waking,
know I dream, and dream myself
into a dream of sleep,
where I am lost in an effortless race
down a darkening street.

Winter:
This is not
what I expected.
I've found a brightening
and little pain.
I am unafraid,
feel no loss, want no goodbyes.
Spring will return.
People who do not this day exist
will create what I shall never know.
Now is not about death.
Now is about my death.

Hurry

Today is his death day. He who was young
becomes one of us in the rain, while rain's tongue
sings his day and we sing. The sky does not weep,
it sings with the rain. So get up from your sleep.

Up, up. It's a day, grey as night's old grey head,
and we must be off and a toast must be said
to his day and be drunk with the rain. Death is bare
and a waste without rain. Brush your teeth, wash your hair,

wrap our gift. We will drive in the rain. Dark as night
though it is, not the night of bright life, not the sight
of keen men. Night of joy. Night of death. He's our Jack.
Now, Jill. Now, it is time. He will never look back.

Out we go, out the door. I've forgotten the key
for the car. The rain rains, the water runs free
in the gutters, your hair all in tangles. Run, run
to our tomb, but laugh. We need rain, not the sun

for his day, this best day of his life. I'm behind
you my dear. Don't fret his wet gift, that the wind
blows your dress tight on your ass. He's a boy
grown old. Your wet dress on your bones is his joy.

Wet or dry we're away, drive off in the dark.
It's his day, full of rain, and we'll make it work.
We'll go to his house, won't mind being warm,
watch him fall to pieces but come to no harm.

The Man Mouth

At seven:
When I am twice as old
as I am now, I'll be fourteen. And someday twenty.
I'll climb years like stickyfooted bugs climb moonbeams.
I'll fly away, be Superman, but now the moon
makes shadows sneak across my bedroom walls.
 I don't like the noise when moths hit on my screen
like kidnappers who want to take me, chop me up.
I won't let them, don't want to know, want my night light.

At sixteen:
There's whiskey on his breath,
but I don't give a damn when I come home and find him
waiting up for me. I spent the evening in the shadow
of my Ford with her and climbed to heaven inside
her garter belt. Sweet Jesus Christ, I came all
over her, tongue in her mouth, her ears, her hair.
In, in, I'd climb in everywhere, like up
a moonbeam, through the hole the moon makes in the sky.

At thirty-two:
The suburbs aren't all bad.
I take the train and subway into work an hour,
enjoy the chance to breathe, the women in
their business clothes. I seem caught up and flying
backward all at once, an endofline life, responsibility.
They say I have my head on right, will go high
as I have nerve to fly, and wings. I've learned to live

with night, would die for one hot wire of light, one dream.

At forty-eight:
New wife, new child, new life,
the life most dream, chauffeured Park Avenue,
beautiful young female under me, curly headed
golden child. I weigh important in others' eyes,
have place and time, while in recurrent dreams I see myself
emaciated, glassyeyed, as if I'd turned to opium
and lie in some back Chinese room with other addicts,
men of no consequence, onesentenceinthenovel men.

At sixty-five:
He's in my eyes,
the doctor with his light, puff of air, his steely heart.
I have glaucoma, cataracts, unfaithful wife,
prodigal son. I'm drawn to death as if death were
water from artesian springs. We old magicians hold
our purse strings visible, let slip gold coins
that disappear noiselessly into moonfilled air, and we,
alive, dead under the moon that falls on everyone.

Old Love

I did not know that you had died,
imagined all was well
and you still walked the desert dawns,
enjoyed the lingering chill

of night, the rising sun, the silent
setting moon, the smell
of grapefruit, orange, and lemon trees,
taut strings of baby quail.

I did not know that you were ill,
imagined you somewhere
drinking coffee, eating scones,
a chocolate covered pear,

or scrambled eggs and fresh baked bread,
a rainbow trout.

That day you left, I did not know
that you would be the first.

Tears for Elaine

Steam from black coffee
blurs my old wife's eyes.
Her best friend died suddenly.
We don't know why,

can't grasp that Elaine
must be forever gone,
not on vacation,
out walking in warm rain.

Kneed

His knee caught me square in the nuts.
I crumbled. Coach got me off the court.
I groaned, sat scrunched on the bleachers.

My own teammate. In a practice. Later
I asked him why. "Because I felt like it."
That's what the bastard said, pastor's

son, God damned Missouri Lutheran.
Fifty years I've fantasized a Billy Budd
punch and the rest of my life in jail.

* * *

I need a morning drink, a fuck, talk
with a stranger off a Russian freighter,
a walk down Front Street, fried eggs

and hash, a Costa Rican cigar, a joint.
All I have to do is get me there, go back
to 1958, transpose me from the Midwest

to San Francisco Bay, escape my birthright
conscience, caution. I would be one who
worked his way to the coast, died there.

* * *

It's three a.m. We knead the loaves, baguettes,

heat the ovens. Our sweat pours on the floor.
We take a break, smoke cigarettes. I reach

for her awhile, return to baking in a world
that might have been, after the draft, before
I lost my manhood in a pile of library books.

Part Five:

Missippissi 1969

A Bullet for Jane Fonda

It's true. My in-law said so. He should know
what happened in those days. They lived on fear,
the radical conservatives who sow

their seed of hatred for the poor, then, go
about fat lives with dignity. It's clear.
It's true. My brother-in-law says so. He'd know

since he was there. Jane planned to break into
an Army jail and free the dopers, queers,
taunt radical conservatives, whackos

who thought she should be dead, vowed to slow
The Great Decline. Jane snarled, but dared not sneer
at my MP-in-law. He said so, would know

the drill. He'd written "JANE" on his ammo,
hoped for a good, clean shot, bulls eye, to cheer
his radical conservatives, who'd sow

God's wrath, fertilize with blood, and grow
cold fear into a wall of thorns. They peered
at change and shuddered. He told me so. He'd know,
my radical conservative, my bro.

Mississippi 1969

Forward

The river is thick with sunk things
that drift south at half
the water's speed, catch on

waterlogged tree limbs,
a pail filled with water,
caught and pulled horizontal,

while a skull drifts by.
It will break free and make it,
buried there, to Mississippi.

Barefoot in summer

An empty can of beans
in the weeds, razor lid attached,
alive with ants, mold, and blood.

Storm

Hardscrabble farm. Dawn air.
Fatback and chicory coffee.
The hound raises its nose.

Too uncoordinated

Silly little black girl
skipping double dutch like crazy.
White kids watch and eat.

Biscuits and

Few things excite like
grease. We kill what we love best
ourselves, our children.

The Larry Lupton trio

There is no such group.
There never was. Yet they play
so well together.

The Self-Made Man

The Self-Made Man at a fine restaurant

The privacy that
riches bring: joy of spending
money on myself.

The Self-Made Man at church

God forgive me for
earning less last year than I
earned the year before.

The Self-Made Man puts steel wool to his crack

My anus tingles
when I think my employees
vote to make me rich.

The Self-Made Man returns

I have not been here
in many years. I see here's
changed, and you. Not I.

The Confederate Soldier Inside Me

Once I jogged in a Confederate cemetery
And felt one of the dead latch onto me,
Make me his home. He wished me well,
Indicated he would be awhile, my boarder, guide.

I was a flake of snow back then, mattered
Not at all to anyone. My ghost was not content
To be a hanger-on in someone fatuous as I.
He convinced me to become a business man

And to succeed, to honor family, the flag, courage,
Honesty. I've grown old, sometimes forget
My tenant. I should go back and walk his cemetery,
Let him slip into his grave, if that were possible.

Could another live in him who lives in me?
Beside the Union bullet in his head? And we are three?
I'll die, and dead, we'll slip inside a child, help it
Succeed and profit from its world. We will be four. Or five.

Dust

A hundred years ago its owner might have
thought, "Our shotgun's beautiful, located
on this lovely Uptown lot. We've painted
it in lavender, chartreuse, and mauve,
furnished half for Grandmama, a slave
Abe freed, bond woman, servant. We created
rooms of sweetness, peace for her, sweated
over what would last beyond our graves."

The house lies paintless, empty, shattered
on a dirt lot tracked with plastic bottles, tires.
The porch, front doors remain, disguise the ghost
inside, wall boards ripped out, ceilings scattered
round the lot, dumpsters full of floors, a pyre
of tiles. A hard hat hoses down the dust.

Acknowledgments

I am grateful to many people who have helped me with my poetry:

The editor of Burlesque Press, Daniel Wallace, spent hours culling printable poems from a large basket of my poetry. He is amazing.

My daughters, Amanda Boyden, Margaret Greteman, and Emily Bihun never flinch at the piles of poems I send them.

The editor of River Styx, Richard Newman, works patiently with me and other senior writers. He's good for us, Pat, Gloria, Ron, Jim, Mary Ruth, and all you others. Thank you, Richard.

Steven Schreiner, another fine poet and teacher, generously gave us his time and critical attention.

Joan Houlihan's Colrain workshop twice gave me the impetus to revise, revise, revise. Colrain is terrific. Try it.

I heard the great poets read at Washington University, where I took my first writing classes from Jennifer Atkinson and Jason Sommer. Mary Jo Bang, I wish I could write and think like you.

Finally, thank you wife Mary Anne and step-children Barb and Rudy for your patience with my bad habit.

About the author

Bill has published about 100 poems in a variety of magazines, including *Callaloo, Christian Century, Collages and Bricolages, Iris, The Laurel Review, Mid American Review, Phoebe, Riprap, River Styx, Sou'Wester, The Madison Review,* and the anthology *Chick for a Day*. His chapbooks are *Jill: a poem in 100 Spenserian Stanzas* (Tamafyhr Mountain Press) and *Imitations* (Chiron Review Press). He holds degrees from Concordia College, Valparaiso University, Northwestern, and Washington University. He lives and writes in St. Lous, MO.